Kenny

JIMMY CARTER

Order this book online at www.trafford.com
or email orders@trafford.com

Most Trafford titles are also available at major online book retailers.

Print information available on the last page.

ISBN: 978-1-4907-6503-7 (sc)
ISBN: 978-1-4907-6505-1 (hc)
ISBN: 978-1-4907-6504-4 (e)

Library of Congress Control Number: 2015914685

Trafford rev. 10/23/2015

Trafford
PUBLISHING® www.trafford.com
North America & international
toll-free: 1 888 232 4444 (USA & Canada)
fax: 812 355 4082

I am dedicating this book to the ladies of the library in Blanco, Texas, who were so helpful to me when I was doing my research.

This book is about Kenneth Harold Anderson, who was drafted into the United States Army in World War II, enduring the horrors of the gory sword of war, as others did in the WORLD Wars and others, experiencing trauma to mind and body that no one should have to go through,, but Kenneth served with courage and honor under the most dreadful and atrocious conditions. While serving in the United States Army, he was awarded the Silver Star; he was awarded two Bronze Stars, he was awarded the prestigious French Croix De Guerre, he was awarded the Purple Heart with Cluster, as he was wounded twice on the battle fields, he had numerous Campaign Ribbons because he participated in many of the major battles fought in the European Theater in World War II. Kenneth was a sergeant who was quiet, reserved, reticent, modest and was reluctant to speak about his experiences and contributions while serving his country, but history speaks for itself-----this is his story.

CHAPTER

One

Kenneth, his friends called him Kenny, was born March 1, 1927, in Terre Haute, Indiana. Terre Haute is a city in Vigo County, near the state's western border with Illinois, seventy-five miles west of Indianapolis, as of the 2000 census, the city had a population of 59,614. The name of the city is derived from the French phrase "terre haute", meaning "high land" it was named by French explorers in the eighteenth century to describe the plateau-like rise of land next to the Wabash River. The construction of Fort Harrison during Tecumshehs War" marked the first known population of European Americans. An Indian Tribe Village called "Weananu", also known as "Rising Sun" already existed near the fort. Captain Zachary Taylor defended the fort against British, inspired six hundred Native Americans during the Battle of Fort Harrison, September 4, 1812. The orchards and meadows kept by the local Wea population became the site of present day Terre Haute a few miles south of Fort. By 1830, the few remaining Wea Indians departed, due to pressure from the white settlement.

The completion of the "Wabash and Erie Canal", The longest man made body of water in the Western Hemisphere, brought prosperity to the area, the canal, along with the "Terre Haute and Indianapolis Railroad", quickly gained the reputation as a transportation hub. Terre Haute's famous "Four-Cornered Race Track" was the site of more than twenty world harness racing records and helped trigger the city's reputation as a sporting center. Terre Haute became a city in 1853. Terre Haute has a sister city relationship with Tajimi, Japan.

Kenneth's childhood development years were spent on his father's farm, near Terre Haute. Every year, Kenneth, his father and brother Leo, armed with axes and saws, would go into the woods to lay-in a large supply of wood to ensure that the family would have enough fuel to sustain their heating and cooking needs during the extreme temperatures of the winters in Indiana. On occasion, a tree that was cut down contained a bee hive, they would gather buckets of honey to take home. The work was hard and exhausting, but Kenneth was always ready, willing and able to do his part, he was also motivated by knowing that his mother would have a sumptuous dinner waiting for them when they got home. Kenneth also participated in the "hog rolling" or butchering of hogs. As many as twenty neighbors would gather in the fall to augment their meat supplies, they would share in the work and meat from the hogs. A neighbor, whose name was Fred Lamb, had only one job, which was to dispatch the hogs quickly and proficiently with the blunt end of an axe. The others scraped the hair off the hogs, butcher them and boil-down the lard. When the butchering was at the Anderson farm, Kenneth's mother would cook a huge meal for the crew, featuring a large platter of pork livers and a special treat, the "cracklings" or pig skins. The events were as much social gatherings as just occasions to obtain meat. To make some money, Kenneth set box traps cottontail rabbits and muskrats, for which he received a dollar for each of their pelts. He also caught fling squirrels, which became pets.

Kenneth attended and graduated from Concanon School, which was a twelve grade school. In the eleventh grade, he cut a finger in wood shop that was so severe that he almost lost his finger and it never healed correctly. He graduated in May of 1938.

Between the years from which he graduated in May 1938 and when he was drafted in May of 1942, Kenneth worked in various jobs, one was as a fireman on the Pennsylvania Railroad. Kenneth was slight of build and it was a hot and energy sapping job. He spent his days shoveling coal into the firebox on the engine, he would come home black from the soot that emitted from the firebox.

Kenneth married his High School sweetheart, Ann Dingle, who was attending St. Mary Of The WOODS COLLEGE in West Terre Haute when they were married. Later in life, Kenneth would often reflect on the etchings on a tombstone that he saw in England: it said "Ann Smith – the children of Isreal wanted food and the Lord sent them manna; old man Smith wanted a wife and the DEVIL sent him Anna".

When he received his draft notice, Kenneth reported to he Induction Center at Fort Harrison, his older brother, Bernard, who had been drafted earlier, was stationed at Fort Harrison as a Military Policeman "MP". Bernard was a "free spirit", who would leave the post whenever he felt like it: often other Military Policemen would be sent to bring him back, but due to tips from friends and family that the MPs were searching for him' Bernard would make it back to the fort before the MPs could catch him. Sometimes he would be locked-up in the brig anyway. When he was released, he would resume his duties until he decided to leave again. The first evening that Kenneth was at the Induction Center, his brother Bernard found him. Bernard said to Kenneth, "Lets go" Kenneth asked "Go where?" Bernard said, "Come on, we are going to town", Kenneth answered, "I am not supposed to leave the post!" Bernard told him, "That's okay, I know how to get on and off the post without being seen". Kenneth reluctantly replied. "Okay". As they departed Fort Harrison, Kenneth thought to himself, "This a very inauspicious start, my first day in the Army and I am already absent without leave!". They went into town, had drinks at several bars and restaurants, then they returned to the post, as Bernard had assured him, they were not caught.

Sometime after Kenneth's first day in the Army, Bernard was attached to a unit whose primary job was to bring German prisoners of war to the United States; the unit, along with relief troops for the North African Campaign, boarded a ship in Norfolk, Virginia, where the ship departed the Continental United States and proceeded to Morocco in Africa. There the relief troops disembarked and the German prisoners were boarded, from there the ship proceed to Algiers to pick-up more German prisoners and then return to the United States. Bernard made two cruises to pick-up prisoners. After that, he returned to Fort Harrison, where he got into an argument with an Army Captain; it isn't clear what the argument was about, but the longer that they talked, the more heated the argument became, finally the Captain said, "I am your Superior Officer and you will do what I tell you to", that was the last straw for Bernard and he decked the Captain. The Captain, who was no match for Bernard, had him arrested and wanted to court marshal him. MPs were dispatched from a facility in Miami, Florida to escort Bernard to that facility. While he was there, by a sheer stroke of luck, Bernard encountered a Colonel that he had previously worked for. The Colonel really liked Bernard and managed to absolve Bernard of all the formal charges that were levied against him. Bernard was honorably discharged shortly after that.

CHAPTER

Two

On the second day that Kenneth was at the Induction Center, he was administered a series of tests, his score on the Intelligence Quotient "IQ" Test was 140, one of the highest scores recorded at the Induction Center. He was immediately dispatched to Emory University in Atlanta, Georgia and was enrolled in the Medical College to begin training for being a doctor in the United States Army. Kenneth studied there for two years; then in 1944, the build -up for D-Day began, Kenneth, along with four others with the highest grade point average who were there in training at the college, were pulled out of college and made instant Front Line Medical Technicians and were sent to Camp Breckenridge in Kentucky, where they participated in maneuvers with other troops in preparation for being shipped out. From there, Kenneth was sent to a British Military facility outside of London, England, where he worked in the Dispensary. The Dispensary did not have a centrifuge, Kenneth helped design and build a centrifuge for the Dispensary. The chief food staple at the Dispensary was "Bully Beef", it was on the menu every day, When Kenneth departed the Dispensary, he declared "I hope I never see bully beef again!"

On June 4, 1944, "Operation Overlord", the allied invasion of Europe was imminent, all the ground troops that were to participate, American and Allied Forces, reported to their ports of embarkation, Kenneth mustered with the American 29th Infantry Division, whose point of attack was to be at Omaha Beach. The 29th Infantry Division was one of the most illustrious outfits of World War II. The Division was engaged in combat almost continuously from D-Day to V-E Day and suffered 20,111 battle casualties in eleven months of combat, over twice the normal manpower compliment of approximately 14,000 men. The Division gained four campaign ribbons for service in the European Theater and was awarded the prestigious Croix de Guerre Avec Palme by the French Government for it's exemplary actions on Omaha Beach on D-Day. The troops were issued a new pair of boots, Kenneth put his on and would not remove them for three weeks, Before the soldiers boarded a troop ship, they were given a motivational speech by General George Patton. After General Patton's speech, the soldiers boarded the Troopships, which was part of a fleet of almost five thousand ships of all kinds, carrying 200,00 sailors, soldiers and Coast Guardsmen. When the word to depart was transmitted to the ships, the fleet cast off mooring lines in unison and proceeded from their ports to assemble at their positions off Normandy's five invasion beaches. Gale force winds buffeted the ships in the English Channel, large swells lifted and lowered the smaller ships like bobbing corks; General Eisenhower felt that he had no choice but to have the ships return to port and hope for better weather for the invasion. The message went out to the ships to turn back, the Destroyers began working like herding dogs, crossing in front of the other ships and guiding them in an effort to turn the tremendously large fleet around and head back to England. The men who had already been living in cramped and uncomfortable conditions would have to wait two more days before their situation would change, most of them will find that living conditions can be worse, a whole lot worse.

The Germans had constructed the most formidably defenses ever known in the history of the world. Using thousands of people as slave labor, millions of tons of concrete had been poured to build machine gun nests; communication trenches, gun emplacements block houses and buildings known as "pill boxes", whose only entrance was a hole on the roof of the buildings, the beaches had been inundated with anti-tank mines, over five million anti-personnel S-mines, nicknamed "Bouncing Bettys" by the Allies, they got their name due to their action of bouncing up from waist to head high and exploding, unleashing a lethal barrage of ball bearings. The beaches were covered with steel and concrete obstacles, topped with teller mines and barbed wire stretching form obstacle to obstacle, off the coast of the beaches, anti-invasion obstacles made of steel, metal tipped wooden stakes and concrete cones topped with mines were placed just below the surface of the water. General Rommel had a large area behind his headquarters flooded and covered with obstacles, barbed wire and mines to protect against an airborne invasion.

General Eisenhower had made his final decision, the Europe invasion would be Tuesday June 6, 1944. Slightly after midnight on June 6, the invasion, which would become known as D-day began. Paratroopers from the 101st and 82nd Divisions began to jump from their aircraft over Normandy, shortly after that, paratroopers from the British 6th Airborne Division jumped in a different location. These were designated "Path Finders" whose job was to light the way for other paratroopers and to clear an area for the glider trains carrying troops; anti-tank guns, heavy equipment and and medical supplies to land. Unfortunately, luck was not with them, due to high winds and unexpected anti-aircraft fire, many did not land in in the intended areas were they were supposed to. The air drops for the eighteen thousand Airborne Troops that followed would prove disastrous for a large number of the men; the glider trains carrying troops from the 101st Airborne Division did not have a large number of casualties, they landed in the areas marked by lights positioned by the Path Finders, the 82nd Airborne Division did not fare as well, most of gliders missed their landing area and crashed, many of the Airborne Troops were killed in the crashes and a large amount of vital supplies that the gliders were carrying was lost. Hundreds of the paratroopers were lost, some missed the coast entirely and were pulled under the water by their heavy equipment and were drowned. Others were lost when they landed in "Rommels Swamp" and were unable to swim or wade out of the muddy waters.

Meanwhile, the ships of the enormous fleet were departing from their various ports and began assembling into formations directed at the assigned beaches where the attack would be launched. British Minesweepers led the way followed by Battleships, Cruisers and Destroyers, trailing them were the Command Ships, Troop Ships and LSTs (Landing Ship Tank).

Kenneth was standing at the railing of a Troop Transport Ship staring at the rough waters that were buffeting the ships, he was apprehensive as to what was his destiny would be and if the operation would be successful. Then he heard the tremendous crescendo of noise from the engines of the big bombers, fighters and other aircraft that filled the skies as they flew over the fleet. He looked up to see wave after wave of aircraft in formation headed for the Normandy coast. The big bombers were supposed to carpet bomb the defensive fortifications simultaneously with the bombardment of shells from the ships to destroy the German gun positions along the coast. The bombers did not accomplish their objective, they dropped their bombs three miles inland from their intended targets.

The ships reached their assigned locations and moved into position. The Minesweepers moved along the coast unseen, having done their job, they headed back out to sea. The Battleships and Cruisers began firing five to six miles from the coast; Battleships Texas and Arkansas fired fourteen inch shells after fourteen inch shells at the one hundred feet high fortification wall on Omaha Beach, the Destroyers were moving along the coast firing one mile out from the shoreline. The ships fired salvo after salvo at the fortifications that had been built along the coast, doing little damage to them. The Germans did not the return the fire that the Americans had been expecting, the Germans were waiting for the assault boats to get in close.

Four artillery batteries of the German 352nd Division were positioned one hundred feet up overlooking Omaha Beach, there were twenty guns of several calibers, including the deadly German 88s, the guns covered one half of the beach. The command bunker was hit, but incredibly, none of the gun bunkers were hit during the extensive shelling of the beach fortifications.

While the ships were firing at the coast, LCIs (Landing Ship Infantry) that carried about thirty men were being lowered to the water from the Troop Ships, some of the boats were loaded with men and equipment before they were lowered over the side, with the ships windlasses; Kenneth was in one of these and the boat was lowered into the water safely, some others were not so lucky, the large waves smashing against the ships caused some of the boats to tip and dump the troops and equipment into the water, causing casualties before they even got started for the beach. On other Troop Ships scramble nets were lowered over the side into the water, after the small boats were lowered into the water, men carrying their heavy equipment would climb down the nets to the boats, some soldiers fell into the boats injuring themselves and others fell into the water.

The landing boats were bobbing around the Troop Ships like corks until all were in the water, then the word was given to begin the assault. As the landing craft were moving toward the beaches, water was washing over the sides of the boats, the men in the boat that Kenneth was in were using their helmets to bail water, trying to keep the landing craft afloat, ten of the of the boats sank off of Omaha Beach because they had taken on too much water. As the boat that Kenneth was in moved closer to the beach, Kenneth saw soldiers in the water, both dead and alive, some of the soldiers were picked-up by rescue boats, others were left to drown.

Twenty-nine amphibious tanks, equipped with large inflatable flotation devices to keep them afloat, were to move onto the beaches to give support to the Special Engineers, who were to destroy mines and obstacles on the beaches and clear paths for the main body of the invasion force who would be coming onto the beaches. LSTs moved in, dropped their loading ramps and the tanks moved out of the boats, all but two of the tanks involved in the initial assault sank into the bay due to the obstacles and missing their assigned landing positions, few of the Special Engineers were able to accomplish their mission. The landing craft that managed to elude the obstacles in the bay came under heavy mortar and machine gun fire, many of the soldiers were cut down when the unloading ramps on the LCIs were dropped and never reached the beach The landing craft that Kenneth was in hit a concrete cone that was topped with a mine and was blown over on it's side, dumping all of it's occupants in the water. Kenneth had a foot locker filled with medical supplies attached to his belt with a lanyard. When he fell into the water, the heavy chest immediately pulled him to the bottom of the bay, Kenneth struggled trying to reach the surface of the water but, with the heavy chest attached, this was an impossible feat, he managed to get his knife out and cut the lanyard that was attached to the heavy weight that was holding him down. He was out of breath when his head emerged above the surface of the water, gasping for air, he began to swim the best he could toward shore, he managed to reach the edge of the beach and fell exhausted there. When Kenneth caught his breath and was able to move, he looked to his right and was staring into the eyes of a dead soldier, other bodies were washing ashore, as other troops were wading onto the beach, to escape the incessant rain of machine gun bullets and mortar shells, some tried to make it to the high concrete wall farther up on the beach, others were taking cover behind the obstacles on the beach and some, with no other cover available, hunkered behind dead bodies. Some of the heroic soldiers, by crawling low to the ground to avoid the machine gun fire, tossed hand grenades into the opening at the top of the pill boxes. The Special Engineers that did make it on the beach had a difficult task, because soldiers had to take cover behind the very obstacles that they were supposed to destroy.

Kenneth looked up to see that there were injured and dead soldiers scattered all over the beach, moving as fast as he could, he moved from one injured soldier to another, improvising the best he could to help them, he tore strips of his own clothing to make bandages, he used belts for tourniquets and rifle stocks for splints. He felt helpless, he had nothing to give the injured soldiers for pain, some were actually vomiting ball bearings and all of his medical supplies were lying at the bottom of the bay.

Kenneth saw an injured soldier moving, previously Kenneth thought he was dead, Kenneth ran to him and turned him over, the soldier gasped Joe! Joe! and pointed to a burning tank. The tank had hit an anti-tank mine and one track was blown off and the tank was on fire, Kenneth ran to the tank and climbed up on top and looked down the hatch into the tank, there was an seriously injured soldier that could not climb out of the tank, Kenneth dropped down into the tank and lifted the soldier to the top of the tank, Kenneth pulled him off of the tank and, amid a hail of machine gun bullets, dragged him to safety behind the concrete wall. The soldier survived the war, but would surely have died if he had been left in the tank. Kenneth received his first Bronze Star for his actions on Omaha Beach.

The second and third wave of the invasion force was more successful. American fighter planes were strafing the arera behind the top of the cliff, Landing Craft were able to push through the obstacles and assault troops stormed ashore, still coming under intense fire from the Gennans, there were many casualties but more attacking soldiers were able to get across the beach, Special Engineers were beginning to eliminate the obstacles on the beach that they were unable to do seven hours earlier. Army Rangers were beginning to scale the cliff and eliminate machine gun nests and other pockets of resistance, ships were firing at the top of the cliff, some of the debris from the shelling was falling on the Rangers, as they climbed toward the top of the cliff. When the Rangers reached the top of the cliff, they took cover in the large craters that were made by the heavy shells from the big Navy guns. Groups of soldiers were taking cover at the base of the high concrete cliff, finally they realized that to stay on the beach would be certain death and started moving out. There were signs sticking out of the sand everywhere that said "Achtung Minen", the soldiers did not have to speak German to know what they meant, because many of the troops had stepped on the mines and were seriously injured. Kenneth was with a group that had found an abandoned German trench and began to move up the cliff using the trench for cover. Before the soldiers reached the top of the cliff, they had to move out of the trench, when they left the trench and started on up the cliff, they came under fire from a German MG 40 machine gun, the soldiers hit the ground looking for the source of the bullets flying at them, they formed an ad hoc assault team and managed to locate and destroy the machine gun nest and capture two German soldiers They made the Germans walk in front of them and stepped exactly where the Germans stepped.

Soldiers from the British 2nd Armies' 41st and 48th Divisions helped secure the beaches. When the day was done, the assault troops were one mile inland, Kenneth would always have the horrifying memory of the cost of taking Omaha Beach, approximately 5,000 casualties was the price that was paid, eventually 9,300 Americans were buried in the cemetery at Omaha Beach.

CHAPTER
Three

The battle for St Lo began on 3 July, continuing on for the next few days with fierce hedgerow fighting. The 29th Infantry Division continued on toward St Lo, which was Headquarters for the powerful German 352nd Division. St Lo is situated on a rocky hill in the lower part of Normandy, the town was originally called "Briovere", meaning Bridge on the Vire River. The German Army occupied the town 17 June 1940, the town is a strategic crossroad in Normandy, the reason the German Army 352nd located their headquarters there.

The countryside was lined with hedgerows, the 29ers came under intense fire from the Germans as they advanced toward St Lo and began to feel like there was a sniper behind every hedgerow, often there was. The 29ers had been marching for fifteen hours straight, when they were joined by an Artillery Unit, the infantrymen were exhausted and hungry because they had run out of provisions. The artillerymen had thirty K-rations, which they gave to the infantrymen, the K-rations were not enough but better than nothing. The 29ers bivouacked in two typical Norman enclosed pastures, the troops were so exhausted that they didn't bother digging foxholes, they simply slumped against hedgerow embankments and immediately fell asleep. The Germans discovered that the 29ers were there and set up MG42 machine guns and sub machine guns behind every hedgerow. The Germans started firing with there automatic weapons and started dropping 120mm mortar rounds in the pastures, they also brought in tank-like assault guns and fired point blank over the hedgerows; the result was a massacre, many of the infantrymen were cut down as they rose to their feet and tumbled in heaps against the hedgerows. Some of the 29ers rallied and knocked -out two of the enemy assault guns with bazookas, but it had little impact on the outcome of the battle. Kenneth grabbed his medical bag and like everyone else, tried to get away from the torrent of machine gun bullets and mortar rounds, he ran for some trees outside of the pasture and ran past a wounded soldier, who cried for help, Kenny turned around and ran back to the wounded man and by pulling the soldier by his arms, managed to drag him out of the pasture away from the shooting. Neither one sustained any more injuries, the wounded man had already suffered being hit by two machine gun bullets. When Kenneth was farther away from the carnage, he treated the soldier's wounds with anti-bacterial sulfa powder and gave him a shot of morphine and attached the syringe to his collar to alert the medics in the rear that he had been given the shot. Kenneth was joined by other stragglers from the ambush who helped him carry the wounded man out of danger. There were about two dozen in all by the time that they reached the 115th Command Post. The wounded men were given further treatment and arrangements were made to have them evacuated to England. Kenneth was finally able to take his boots off, his boots and his feet were a mess, Kenneth was awarded his second Bronze star for his actions during the Germans ambush.

Hundreds of stragglers from the 2nd Battalion, who had been fighting on different fronts, drifted into American lines during the afternoon of June 10 and were reorganized, Kenneth was included in the reorganization. In order to reach St Lo, the 29ers had to cross the Elle River, not much of a river, but the Germans had elected to make a stand there. The 110th Artillery had arrived and aimed their howitzers at suitable targets south of the Elle River. The attack began, hundreds of shells from the American guns hammered the hedgerows south of the Elle, accomplishing very little, the Germans had dug into the hedgerows and their deep slit trenches and dugouts protected them from the artillery bombardment. The Germans had registered their their howitzers and mortars north of the river and the whole area was covered by MG42 machine guns. The American infantry launched their attack 5:00 A.M., they were met by such intense fire that by 10:00 A.M. No one had gotten in ten feet of the river, the unit had suffered 100 casualties. There were so many dead and wounded that Kenneth and other Medical Technicians lost count of how many wounded soldiers that they had attended to. One company managed to cross the Elle but the Americans came under such an intense counter attack by the Germans that they had to retreat back across the river. The 29ers tried again to cross the Elle, but once again they could not breach the German defenses, suffering many more casualties and had to fall back again. The 29th Infantry Division was joined by the 1st and 4th Infantry Divisions and the 2nd and 5th Ranger Battalions. On 15 June 1944, the 30th Infantry Division was subjected to it's baptism of fire in a sector previously occupied by the 501st Parachute Infantry Regiment of the 101st Airborne Division. The American generals in command had under estimated the fierceness that the the Germans would defend St Lo, the 29ers and others began attacking the city on several fronts and were beaten back, one company had so many dead and wounded that they could not continue to fight and had to surrender to the Germans. A few small communities were liberated, one was St Jean-de-Daye, but the Americans could not penetrate into St Lo. The Americans were able to make it to a high ground, which became known as "Hill 108", it also became known as "Purple Heart Hill". When the troops arrived at the top of of the hill, the Germans began shelling the hill with howitzers and mortars. The ground fighting was fierce, often the two armies were battling each other from opposite sides of a hedgerow. Kenneth and another Medical Technician had attended to so many wounded soldiers that they lost count of the casualties. By late afternoon, they were barely able to maintain their position on the hill. When it was obvious that 29ers could not take the city that day, General Bradley called a halt to the offensive. On July 19, 1944, the unit was relieved by the 3rd Battalion; shortly after that the battle at Hill 108 was over, both sides were too exhausted to continue to fight, the 1st Battalion had suffered 250 casualties and had been reduced to forty officers and 308 enlisted men, forty per cent of their strength had been wounded and evacuated. Everyone involved in the battle for St Lo was eventually awarded a Presidential Unit Citation for their stand on Hill 108. After a massive assault by Armored and Infantry Divisions, the Americans were able to fight their way into St Lo, fighting skirmish after skirmish, the infantry began driving the Germans out of St Lo. After the Germans pulled out of the city, they began a salvo of shells from their 88s. The shelling was so intense that the Americans had to keep moving to avoid being hit. The 29th Artillery Division retaliated and were able to silence the 88s. The American Army was able to secure St Lo by late 20 July, the 29th Infantry Division had suffered as many casualties taking St lo as they did on Omaha

Beach. St Lo was almost completely destroyed from shelling from the big guns on both sides, one of the few buildings left standing was the Notre Dame Church built from the thirteenth to fifteenth centuries.

The United States Army had a giant pool of unattached replacements standing by, by replacing soldiers who had become casualties with fresh troops, the unit could stay on the front lines indefinitely. The 29th Infantry Division had been in battle constantly after storming Omaha Beach. Kenneth, like other infantrymen who may have survived the dreadful continuous combat, did not get a break and were completely exhausted.

CHAPTER

Four

O n August 16 and 17 1944, the 29ers pulled into their rest camps, at last the war veterans could get some long needed rest and relaxation; their tranquil time that they were enjoying would be short lived.

General Eisenhower considered Omaha Beach inadequate to bring in the enormous amount of supplies, munitions and troops that would be needed to defeat Hitler's army. General Eisenhower concluded that it was vital to take the port of Brest in Brittany. The Germans also knew that it was vital to prevent the Allies from delivering the war materials at this port and they had a submarine base there. The Germans set-up defenses at all possible entrance ways into Brest; concrete pill boxes, barbed wire barriers, machine gun nests and lengthy anti-tank trenches and had set-up stronger static fortifications at fall back positions. The Germans gathered all outlying units that were in Western Brittany and brought in their exceptional paratroops to defend the area.

Brest is located in a sheltered area not far from the tip of the Breton Peninsula, the largest city in that part of Brittany, a former province of Northwest France.

On August 21, 1944, the 29ers, after only five days rest, were ordered to go to Brest; they were loaded up in trucks and began their journey to where they would encounter the toughest fighting that they would endure in all of World War II. The Commanding General of the 29th Infantry Division was General Hunter Gerhardt Jr., who would have to move 14,000 men and their equipment more than two hundred miles over inadequate roads, with the ever present possibility of an enemy attack, by the morning of August 13, 1944. General Gerhardt had two generals that he had to answer to, one was General Omar Bradley, the other one and his immediate boss was General George Patton, who didn't have much interest in Brest, because the glory was not there; while the 29th Infantry Division was heading for Brest, he was going the other way toward Paris, France, consequently the supplies, especially ammunition was inadequate for the assault on Brest. The 2nd and 8th Infantry Divisions were also ordered to Brest, although three Infantry Divisions were involved, the Americans did not have an advantage in numbers. The American Intelligence's estimate of the strength of German troops at Brest was 16,000 to 20,000, The French Resistance's estimate was 40,000 to 50,000, the French Resistance's estimate was accurate.

The 29th Infantry Division got underway on August 22, 1944. Kenneth looked out of the deuce and a half that he was riding in and mused to himself, "This line of trucks looks like a giant snake", it stretched for forty miles. He looked up to see a piper L-4 "Grasshopper" aircraft flying overhead, relaying any sign of trouble to the ground forces below.

At first the convoy moved along at a pretty good speed but then they caught-up with the traffic; as large as the 29th Infantry

Division was, there were more troops and supplies headed for others areas in France, troops and large flatbed trucks loaded with supplies and ammunition were coming up from Normandy and empty vehicles were bounding south back to Normandy. The traffic was so thick that the convoy could hardly cut in, causing many delays. Kenneth said to himself, "Traffic here is worse than in Atlanta." When the 29ers reached the crossroads at St Halaire du Harcouet, nearly all the vehicles on the road that the 29th was on were turning left toward Paris, while the 29th Division was headed in the opposite direction toward Brittany. After the 29ers left the congested roads, they bounced along at a fairly rapid pace, only slowing down as they passed through the small villages. The roads were lined with smiling, grateful people, who gave them gifts of food, a woman handed three bottles of wine and a basket of eggs to Kenneth. Speaking to the troops that was in the truck he was in, Kenneth asked, "Does anyone of you guys speak French?", someone replied, "French hell, we don't even speak good English", Kenneth turned to the woman and said, "Thank you" and hoped that she understood. Kenneth did not know any of the soldiers that he was traveling with, most of the thousands of 29ers that he was with when they invaded Omaha Beach were dead or wounded, a few were stationed in rear positions, any medics that were on the front lines did not get a break, trained Front Line Medical Technicians were scarce.

As the convoy moved closer to Brest, the 29ers did not like what they were seeing, the countryside was strikingly similar to the terrain that they had been fighting in at St Lo and Vire, the fields were surrounded by stout earthen banks topped by hedges and scrubs, there is no better place to set-up defenses.

The Air Force dropped leaflets on Brest, with the message to the Germans that their position was hopeless but the lives of any German soldiers that surrendered would be spared; the leaflets did not change the mindset of the Germans. The German Commander for the defense of Brest was General Hermann-Bernhard Ramche, who had served in the German Navy, Army and Air Force; the General inspired the German defenders by telling them "We will fight to the last man, bullet and grenade for the glory of our country." General Ramche was not a fanatic; he knew what the fate of himself and his German Military would be, he wanted the defense of Brest to be a delaying action while the German forces in other parts of the European Theater were preparing their offensives. The Germans fought ferociously and it took more than three weeks of continuous fighting for the Americans, with the help of British "Crocodile Tanks" to capture Brest. On the night of 25 August, RAF heavy bombers bombed Brest but they were not sure what their targets were and the bombing did no damage to the concrete structures in Brest. On August 26, the attack on Brest began; the 29ers were ordered to push straight ahead towards Brest. At first, the 29ers could not locate the German forces defending Brest, they concealed machine guns in the hedgerows; when the American troops came into view in the open fields, the Germans would would fire at point blank with machine guns and rifles and then would move to another position, the 29ers were never sure where the enemy would pop-up next. The American troops suffered 1,300 casualties in the first ten days of fighting, there were so many soldiers killed that a temporary cemetery had to be constructed. The Rifle Company that Kenneth was with was hit hard, many in the Rifle Company were either killed or wounded, a Rifle Company of that size usually has six officers, all of the officers in this company were either killed or wounded and command was taken over by a Technical Sergeant, who subsequently was wounded and awarded the Silver Star for his actions. One soldier who had been hit in the thigh and his forehead had been grazed by a bullet was lying on the ground, blood pouring into his eyes, was shouting, "Help me". Kenneth Picked him up in a fireman carry and started out of the field of fire, when he was hit in the foot by a K98K Mauser and went down. Kenneth began crawling and dragging the wounded soldier out of the clearing, when two soldiers risking their lives, helped Kenneth and the wounded man out of the clearing. Kenneth was taken, with others, to a medical station in the rear where medical personnel attended to their wounds and then made arrangements for evacuations to the 279th Hospital in Wales. Kenneth arrived at the hospital exhausted physically and suffering from "battle fatigue" and his mental state was a disaster, his days were brightened by the prescience of Second Lieutenant Claire H. Ritchie, her nickname was "Adgy", who was from Boston Massachusetts. The lieutenant's duties brought her to the ward every day, her cheerful countenance and friendly manner was a little beam of sunshine to the wounded men,

When the doctors determined that Kenneth could walk on his wounded foot okay, he was transferred to the Rehabilitation Unit at the hospital, where he was given "Narco Therapy", he was given extremely strong tranquilizers nicknamed "Blue 88s" after the big German guns. The tranquilizers took the war and just about everything else off Kenneth's mind, he became the ward of Kevin G. Voit, who took him to therapy; chow, to the shower, to bed and any other place that he had to go. Kevin G. Voit who had recently returned from the front was waiting to be awarded the Bronze Star and a Presidential Citation and was considered to be one of the Army's best Platoon Sergeants. As the days passed, Kenneth was given fewer of the tranquilizers and then was taken off of them all together. Since Kenneth was a trained Medical Technician, he joined the Medical Staff and took care of a wounded soldier, as Sergeant Voit had done for him. Kenneth's stay at the hospital was not for long, however, because he received orders to go back to the front.

CHAPTER

Five

K enneth was assigned to the 28th Infantry Division. The 28th Infantry Division is a unit of the Army National Guard and is the oldest Infantry Division in the armed forces of the United States. The Division was established in 1879 and was later designated the 28th Infantry Division in 1917 after America's entry into World War 1, the 28th Infantry Division is nicknamed the "Keystone Division", as it was formed from units of the Pennsylvania National Guard, Pennsylvania is known as the "Keystone State". The 28th Infantry Division was ordered into federal service February 17, 1941 for one year of active duty; the attack on Pearl harbor by the Japanese on December 7, 1941 caused soldiers of the 28th Infantry Division to remain on active duty for the duration of the war.

The 28th Infantry Division trained for ten months in England and Wales, then entered combat July 22. 1944, landing on the beaches of Normandy. After the United States and Allied Troops stormed the Normandy beaches June 6, 1944, the 28th

Infantry Division advanced across Western France, including Percy; Montbray, Monyguoray and Sever de Caldovas. The 28th Infantry Division, fighting with XIX Corps, secured the western most Falaise Gap. The Falaise Gap was in lower Normandy, France. British and Canadian Forces were coming from the north, United States Forces were coming from the south. The Germans tried to escape by going through the gap; they tried to cross the Dives River in and around the town of Chambois. The Dives River is a 105 KM long river in Normandy that flows into the English Channel in Cabourg, when the German soldiers tried to cross the river, they were cut off and were decimated, the Allies captured 38,000 German soldiers

In late August, The Division was moving along Seine River, the Seine River is 776 kilometers long and is an important commercial waterway within the Paris Basin in the north of France. The 28th Infantry Division succeeded in trapping the remnant of the German 7th Army throughout Vorneuil, Breteui, Damvile, Conch, Le Neuborg and Elbeuf. On August 29, 1944 the Division paraded through Paris, France to join in their liberation celebration, from there the Division continued on to to the border of Germany, where they would be in some of the most bloody battles of the war. The fury of the attacks by the 28th Infantry Division led the Germans to bestow the name "Bloody Bucket Division" on them.

The 28th Infantry Division continued it's advance through the Forest of Compeigne, which is a large forest thirty-seven miles (60 km) in an area 60 km north of Paris. The 28th continued on to La Fere; St Quentin, Laon, Sedan, Mezieres, Bouillon and eventually across the Meuse River into Belgium. The Meuse River is a major waterway in Europe, flowing northward 590 miles (950 km) from the Langres Plateau in France and through Belgium and the Netherlands to the North Sea. The 28th Infantry Division averaged seventeen miles a day against heavy resistance from German battle groups. In early September, after capturing the city of Arlon, Belgium, the Division fanned out into Luxembourg. On September, 1944, the 28th was the first American unit to enter Germany.

The 28th Infantry Division gegan assaults, which destroyed or captured 153 pillboxes and bunkers, then the Division moved north, clearing the Monchau Forest of German forces. The Division had a brief rest and then made another move northward to the Huertgen Forest, in late September.

Kenneth was directed to report to a staging area, where other replacement infantry soldiers, some that were also going to the 28th Infantry Division had gathered waiting for transportation to France. Kenneth was informed that his "Limousine is here", the limousine was actually a 1942 Ford ambulance. He was was issued a medical bag, then he walked out of the doors of the hospital and climbed into the ambulance. He was driven to the staging area by Adeline, better known as "Adgy" Fernwalter, Adeline was an attractive, friendly person, whose cheerfulness had gained everyone's respect and admiration. When they arrived at the staging area, Adeline leaned over and kissed Kenneth and said softly, "Good Luck Kenny", he replied, "Good luck to you too Adgy", then he stepped out of the ambulance and walked away without looking back.

Kenneth observed the mob that had gathered there, he estimated that there were about 2000 soldiers milling around in organized confusion, waiting for orders to board the Troop Ships. When the order came, the soldiers began filing aboard the ships. When everyone had boarded, mooring lines were cast-off and the ships began moving away from the piers. The Troop Ships joined with Supply Ships and other Naval ships forming a convoy. Mine Sweepers led the way, six American Destroyers moved into position, which was a large circle around the convoy, forming a screen to protect the convoy from any German Submarines that might be in the area.

Kenneth walked out on the deck and looked up at the empty skies; he recalled the last time that he had made this voyage, the skies were filled with hundreds of aircraft, he remembered the crescendo of noise made by the aircraft as they began flying over, the buzz of the escort fighters and the ominous roar of the big bombers throats. He looked at the white caps and remembered all of the seasick soldiers lining the rails of the Troop Ships, he hooped that this wouldn't happen this time.

As Kenneth was looking out over the turbulent water, he was joined by a Corporal Price, Corporal Price was about five feet ten inches tall, with a swarthy complexion, dark hair and dark brown eyes. Corporal Price asked Kenneth, "Were you with the invasion force on June 6th?" Kenneth replied, "Yes I was?" Corporal Price said, "I heard that it was a disaster". Kenneth said, "I try to forget about it". Kenneth asked Corporal Price "Do you have any idea where are supposed to go when we get to Normandy?", Corporal Price replied, "I don't have a clue!", Kenneth said, "Neither do I."

As the convoy neared it's destination, unpleasant thoughts raced through Kenneth's mind; he remembered all the things that went wrong on June 6th, The bombers missing their targets, Paratroops and gliders being dropped in the wrong zones, many Paratroopers drowned in the swamps, without firing a shot, the Special Engineers being unable to get onto the beaches to remove the myriad of obstacles and mines, the floating tanks that were supposed to support the troops coming onto the beaches sinking before they reached the shore. He remembered the landing craft that he was in being blown over by a mine and the heavy medical chest pulling him to the bottom of the water, his struggle to cut the lanyard and get to the top of the water to get some air. Then the horrors he encountered when he reached the beach; destruction and waste everywhere, dead and and wounded soldiers were scattered all over the beach, the incessant hail of bullets from MG42 machine guns nicknamed "Hitler's Buzzsaw" and the powerful German 88 Howitzers firing point blank at the soldiers coming off of the landing crafts. He recalled trying to get through the barbed wire to get to the wounded soldiers and trying to administer to them without any medical equipment, taking cover behind dead soldiers because there was no other cover available. The only tank that had reached Omaha Beach had been blown off of it's tracks and was on fire. 5000 American fighting men died, he didn't know how many of our Allies were killed in the battle. He wondered. "How many more brilliant operations will I have to survive"?

When the ships reached their destination, they anchored and the Troop Ships started lowering the Landing Craft Infantry (LCIs) into the water, the soldiers began climbing down into them for their final leg to the beach, meanwhile the Supply Ships were unloading their cargo. When the landing craft that Kenneth was in reached the beach, he and Corporal started walking up the beach together, they observed a long line of trucks on the beach and walked over to where they were at. There they encountered a Warrant Officer, who was about forty-five years of age, with graying hair and mustache and a haggard look on his face. He was being bombarded with questions that he could not answer, finally, he climbed onto one of the trucks and shouted, "Just ask the drivers where they are going!" then he jumped down and went some place that he couldn't be found.

Kenneth and Corporal Price started walking down the line of trucks asking the drivers where they were going, some of them didn't seem to know, finally they came to a Tech Sergeant Roberts, who was about five feet ten inches tall, a little on the chubby side, with sandy hair and wearing horn- glasses. Kenneth asked him, "Are you going to the 28th Infantry Division?" The sergeant replied, "I think so, the last that I heard, they were in the east, we are going to drive up there and hope to find them before the Germans blow us off the road". With little confidence, Kenneth and Corporal price climbed into the truck. There was a lengthy wait while Sergeant Roberts conferred with some other drivers. Little by little other Replacement Troops began climbing into the trucks. Finally, as other trucks were pulling out, five trucks loaded with Replacement Troops, ammunition, food and other supplies were on their way to Eastern France.

As the trucks bumped along to Eastern France, Kenneth and Corporal Price had lots of time to talk. Corporal Price showed Kenneth pictures of his wife and children, who lived in Seattle, Washington, Kenneth said, "I have a daughter but it has been a long time since I have seen her or even heard anything from her mother, probably the only way I could hear from her is to stop my allotment to her, then I would hear from her". Corporal Price said, "I would like for you to come and visit us in Washington, when this war is over", Kenneth replied, "I would like that".

The trucks stopped at a check point near Amiens, France. When a Military Policeman (MP) came to the window of the truck that Sergeant Roberts was driving, the Sergeant asked the MP, "Is the 28th Infantry Division anywhere around here?", the MP replied, "No, the last time that I heard anything about them, they had crossed the Meuse River into Belgium. The Meuse River is a major European waterway, rising in France and flowing through Belgium and the Netherlands before draining into the North Sea, it has a total length of 925 km (575 miles), the Meuse is the oldest river in the world.

Sergeant Roberts thanked the MP and climbed out of his truck and went back to have a conference with the other drivers. The drivers checked their maps and then climbed back back into their trucks and headed for Belgium. The trucks crossed the border and stopped in Namur, Belgium. A Radioman in one of the trucks kept trying desperately to contact anyone that he could to get some information, finally, he learned that the 28th had crossed Luxembourg into Germany. The truck drivers stopped and had another conference, checked their maps, then climbed back into their trucks and rolled on toward Luxembourg.

The trucks kept going until they crossed out of Belgium into Luxembourg, they rolled on until came to Mersch, Luxembourg, where they stopped for a "bathroom call"; while they were there, they had a good meal at a restaurant, the first good meal that they had eaten in days. When they had finished eating, the troops climbed back into the trucks and continued on to Germany, the Radioman was able to contact General Norman "Dutch" Cota's Headquarters and get directions as to where they should go. The trucks continued on down the road until they caught up with the 28th Infantry Division near the Huertgen Forest on September 30, 1944. The Huertgen Forest stretches north-east from the Belgium-German border covering an area of about fifty square miles from the triangle formed by the towns of Aachen, Dueren and Monschau. The terrain of the Huertgen Forest is characterized by plunging valleys that carve through broad plateaus, the Huertgen Forest is thickly wooded and the hilltops have been cleared for agriculture, roads in the forest are few, the ones that are there and are winding and narrow.

The Replacement Troops and supplies were welcomed by the 28th Infantry Division because they were running low on almost everything and had suffered heavy losses in some of the battles. Kenneth and Corporal Price were assigned to the 109th Infantry Regiment. On November 2, 1944, Kenneth and Corporal Price were members of an Observation Patrol that entered the Huertgen Forrest, their mission was not to engage the enemy but to locate German troops and armor. They moved through the woods for about a hour, then quietly left the heavily wooded area and walked out into a clearing: the silence was broken by a sound Kenneth was all too familiar with, the sound of a MG42 machine gun firing at the patrol, soldiers began to fall. In the midst of a rain of bullets, Kenneth ran to the first man that had fallen, knelt and examined the soldier and realized that he was dead. He quickly got to his feet and ran to a sergeant who had fallen clutching his 45 caliber Thompson Sub Machine Gun to his chest, the sergeant had been hit twice in his shoulder with machine gun bullets, Kenneth applied a pressure bandage to the wounded man's shoulder and secured his arm to his body with a sling and gave him a shot of morphine and attached the syringe to his collar. A Bazookaman that was with the patrol located the machine gun nest and with an accurate shot, silenced it. The impact of bullets striking the ground from German Soldiers firing their Kar.98k Mausers were still raining down around Kenneth and the sergeant. Kenneth looked up to see three German Soldiers emerging from the woods, firing their rifles at the Americans, he quickly picked- up the sergeants Thompson and began spraying bullets at the Germans, two of the Germans fell and the other one fled into the woods. Private First Class (PFC) Skelly came out and quickly got into the prone position and began peppering the woods with bullets from his 30 caliber belt fed M1919A6 light machine gun, PFC Skelly kept the Germans at bay long enough for Kenneth to lift the sergeant into a "Firemans Carry" and get him to safety, while other soldiers were helping other wounded men to get clear of the area. Kenneth patched-up the wounded soldiers the best that he could and arranged to have them transported to a Medical-Aid Station in the rear, where they would be treated by Lieutenant Bedford Davis, 2nd Battalion Surgeon. Kenneth was awarded the Silver Star for is actions while under fire from the enemy.

That night, over come with emotion, Kenneth screamed as loud as he could, "I hate this war!", his new and only close friend, Corporal Price was killed in the attack.

The 28th Infantry Division stormed into battle amid savage fighting and heavy losses; the battle was centered around the small towns of Vossenack, Kommerscheidt and Schmidt. The 110th Regiment advanced through the forest, taking cover trees, lying in a prone position firing their M1 Rifles at an unseen enemy. It became a seesaw battle, with each side beating the other back and no one gaining an advantage. On November 3, 1944, the 112th Infantry Regiment took Schmidt, the Germans immediately launched a counter attack and the 112th Infantry Regiment was beaten back. On November 10, 1944, the 28th Infantry Division gathered their equipment and wounded and began to move south. Other Infantry Divisions and Armor Divisions and the 82nd Airborne Division continued the battle of the forest. The Germans held the Allied Offensive to a dead standstill for three months, while a few miles south three German field armies assembled in almost complete secrecy for the Ardennes offensive. In the battle in the forest, more than 24,00 Americans were killed, wounded, missing or were captured, another 9,000 succumbed to trench foot, respiratory diseases and combat fatigue.

On November 10, the 28th Infantry Division began their move to the south, the 28th held a twenty-five mile sector of the front line along the Our River. The Our River is a left tributary to the river Sauer/Sure. The river has a total length of 78 kilometers (48 Miles). Kenneth went with the 110th Infantry Regiment to the corridor of Bastogne, Belgium. Kenneth's unit was stationed near Germund and Marnach.

On the other side of the our River, the Germans had assembled three entire armies, the 6th and 5th Panzers and the 7th Army. The three armies comprised thirty Divisions, which was a quarter of a million men; hundreds of tanks, hundreds of self-propelled guns, thousands of trucks, half tracks, armored cars and other vehicles. The Luftwaffe had assembled one thousand airplanes for this operation.

On December 15, 1944, Kenneth was with an observation patrol. The patrol was above the Our River, the patrol found a position from which they could watch the river; they observed the river and surrounding area for about an hour, having not seen anything, they moved closer to the river, suddenly they stopped because they could hear the sound of motors coming from the river. They stealthily moved closer to the river for a better look, the Germans were building a bridge across the river, it was a foot under the water but timbers were being put into place. The patrol quickly hurried back and reported what they had seen, but no one seemed particularly concerned. The patrol began to dig foxholes and prepare for a cold snowy night, envying those who had a roof over their heads this night.

Sergeant Wilson and others were temporarily staying at a hotel in Marnach, something the Hotel Proprietor wasn't too pleased about. There was a man in a wheelchair staying at the hotel also. Sergeant Wilson couldn't determine the man's nationality but he seemed to be a cordial person.

On December 16, 1944, "The Battle Of The Bulge" or as the Germans called it, "Operation Herbstnebel" began. At 0530, the Germans began crossing the Our River in mass by using boats and bridges that they had constructed and then they started infiltrating the countryside.

At 0600, Sergeant Wilson and others, including the wheelchair bound man were in the lobby of the hotel. The sound of the Germans firing their big guns startled everyone. The Hotel Proprietor slipped a nine millimeter Luger pistol to the man in the wheelchair, who began firing immediately at the American soldiers, hitting a Private in the back; Sergeant Wilson quickly kicked the wheelchair over and took the pistol from the man lying on the floor and hit the Hotel Proprietor on the head with it, knocking him unconscious. The Sergeant picked-up the wounded Private and yelled, "Get everyone out of here", the other soldiers, who were already alerted by the sound of the big guns firing were already on the move and began quickly evacuating the hotel.

Sergeant Wilson carried the Private to his jeep, which was parked outside and placed the Private in it, while the other soldiers piled all over the jeep. They left immediately, wanting to get clear of the city. As the jeep bumped along, large caliber artillery shells began hammering the hotel that the soldiers had stayed in and other buildings in the city, soon they were reduced to a pile of rubble.

The Sergeant drove to an area where other members of the 110th Infantry Regiment were dug in, the soldiers quickly began digging foxholes and slit trenches. The Sergeant found Kenneth and brought him to look at the Private. Kenneth examined the Private, but his eyes had already glazed over, all Kenneth could do was shake his head and retrieve a body bag.

The Germans, who greatly outnumbered the 28th Infantry Division, began attacking all along the front. The goal of the German offensive was to gain control of the harbor at Antwerp, Belgium. In order to reach Antwerp before the Allies could regroup, German mechanized force had to seize the roadways trough eastern Belgium, because all seven main roads in the Ardennes Mountain Range converged at the small town of Bastogne, Belgium. Their plan was to take Bastogne quickly and move on down to the Muese River.

Most of the buildings in Marnach were either blown up or burned from incendiary artillery shells. The situation was the same in Wiltz, the home of the 28th Infantry Division's Headquarters, about all communications were almost completely knocked-out. The initial shelling from the German's artillery guns lasted about an hour, by 0630, most of the shelling had stopped.

The Soldiers of the 110th Infantry Regiment could hear movement from the German foot soldiers, but visibility was minimum. The 110th set-up one fifty caliber machine gun and two water-cooled thirty caliber machine guns. When the fog began to lift, the men had an excellent view of the German soldiers, there were multiple targets to choose from, the Americans started firing and the Germans began to fall like dominos, the 109th Field Artillery began to saturate the approaches to Marnach with shells from their 105 millimeter Howitzers, the German Infantry was coming at the men of the 110th in waves of twenty and thirty abreast, the artillery slaughtered the enemy soldiers, the ones who got through the artillery barrage were shot down by machine gun and rifle fire. The German Infantry kept coming out of the woods one wave after the other, the area became a field of bodies as the German foot soldiers were massacred. German artillery fire also kept raining into Marnach. Sergeant Kuhn and Lieutenant Carson were checking on their men when an artillery shell exploded near them and a piece of shrapnel took a big gash out of lieutenant Carson's wrist. Sergeant Kuhn immediately found Kenneth, who bandaged the wound and gave him antibiotics. Kenneth told Sergeant Kuhn that the lieutenant needed to be hospitalized; Sergeant Kuhn put Lieutenant Carson into a jeep and told the driver to take him to the Regimental aid station. Kenneth and other Medical Technicians were kept busy attending to soldiers with shrapnel wounds and disabled with concussions caused by the exploding artillery shells.

As the Lieutenant's jeep was departing, hundreds of German infantry soldiers were bypassing Marnach, unable to take Marnach, they started surrounding the city. To the south, the

Germans were launching a major attack on Hosingen; Weiler, Holtzthum and Consthum. The Americans were holding on at Consthum, The American soldiers brought in Quad Fifty Caliber Machine Guns, the machine guns were designed to shoot down enemy aircraft, but were particularly devastating weapons against infantry. The machine guns tore the enemy soldiers apart as they attacked. The Americans also brought in two 57 millimeter guns, firing high explosive anti-personnel shells, the guns were especially effective stopping attacks by the Germans. Using these weapons and other arms, the Americans, outnumbered five to one, repelled five attacks by the Germans.

About noon, the Germans finished building two bridges across the Our River, German tanks and half-tracks began to stream across the river. The men of the 110th Infantry Regiment heard the tanks, but all they had to defend against tanks were mortars and one anti-tank gun, they requested artillery support, but there wasn't any artillery support available. A jeep pulling a trailer full of mortar ammunition managed to get into the city, the mortar shells were quickly unloaded and the jeep left. Five German tanks and scores of German Infantrymen came in to view. The Americans managed to knock-out two German tanks, but the others kept coming. The German soldiers were being knocked down like bowling pins, but the German infantrymen and tanks kept coming. Soldiers on the outskirts of Marnach were surrounded and running out of ammunition, the same thing was happening in other small towns around Bastogne.

A tank with a flame thrower closed in on the defenders that were dug-in around Marnach; the tank began torching the foxholes, almost all of the defenders were either killed or captured, some were burned alive. Kenneth and other members of the observation Patrol took refuge in a two story building in Marnach, they were firing out of the building's windows at the German soldiers when three tanks entered the city, one of the tanks stopped in front of the building that the soldiers were in, the tank's turret turned and the big gun was aimed point blank at the building. There was a back door to the building, the soldiers quickly scrambled out the door and ran up a hill into some pine trees.

Kenneth and other soldiers who were defending Marnach and from other towns that that had been overrun by the Germans made it to Clervaux. Kenneth went to a temporary hospital that had been set up, there he and other Medical Technicians were kept busy caring for a steady stream of wounded soldiers; some had broken bones from bullets and the impact of the explosions from artillery shells, many had shrapnel wounds, some whose guts were being held in by temporary bandages. As the Germans closed in on the city, the temporary hospital was abandoned.

There was a feudal castle there with origins in the twelfth century. It was a sturdy building several stories high, with many apertures that made excellent firing stations for the defending soldiers inside, any German soldiers within range of the castle were in danger of being shot, there were dead Germans all around the castle. The wounded soldiers, along with civilians and German prisoners were moved into the basement of the castle. The defending soldiers wanted to make a withdrawal, but the streets were jammed with German vehicles and foot soldiers, making a withdrawal impossible. German tanks fired artillery shells at the castle, but all that they accomplished was knocking chunks out of the sides of the building and didn't cause any major damage. The Germans brought in two self-propelled 88 millimeter Howitzersa, they started firing incendiary shells at the roof of the castle, starting some fires. The American soldiers held out in the castle for three days, then ran out of ammunition, with nothing left to fight with, the decision was made to surrender.

When the order to surrender came, Kenneth was in the basement changing the bandage on one of twelve Army Rangers, who had been in almost constant battle for days. One of the Rangers said, "We ain't going to do it!" The Rangers and Kenneth left through one of the doors of the castle, evaded the Germans and ran for cover. They made their way north, marching through chilly rain and mud. They saw a column of trucks and half-tracks they recognized as being American, slipping and sliding, they ran toward the column shouting as loud as they could. Part of the column slowed down and the soldiers were able to catch up with them. The soldiers in the vehicles helped the running men get aboard. The column of vehicles was part of the Headquarters Company 20th Armored Infantry battalion, their destination was Bastogne. Kenneth was in a half-track, he was glad to be in anything that was getting him out of the area, but there was a foot of mud on the road and the tires of the vehicle ahead of the half-track kept throwing mud over everything, including the passengers and the wind and rain was cold.

By the time that the members of the 20th Armored Infantry battalion reached Bastogne, the 110th Infantry Regiment had been reduced to the stragglers that had managed to make it to Bastogne. Cooks, clerks and some medics had been drafted as combat soldiers, some didn't even know how to load their weapons. Sergeant Major Simmons was summoned to the Command Post, where he was issued some shoulder patches and instructed to find everyone that he could and tell them to take off their shoulder patches and sew on the new ones. There were a lot of German spies in Bastogne, the command was hoping that the German spies would see the patches and report to Germans that were attacking that fresh troops had arrived in Bastogne to defend the city.

On December 19, 1944, the Germans organized a major attack on the village of Norville. The attack was repelled by M18 Hellcat Tank Destroyers, the Hellcats were more maneuverable than the German tanks, with a top speed of fifty-five miles per hour they confused the Germans and destroyed many tanks. On 20 December, 1944, the 101st Airborne formed an all around perimeter on the northwest shoulder of the city to block the Germans from gaining control of the road to Bastogne. Three Artillery Battalions were commandeered and formed a temporary Artillery Group. The 969th Field Artillery Battalion was part of the Artillery Group. The 969th was an all black Battalion, whose accuracy with their 155 millimeter Howitzers was legendary.

The Germans knew that they had to take Norville in order to take the road to Bastogne, they organized another massive attack, tank and artillery shells rained down on the village. The 101st Airborne suffered heavy losses, there so many wounded paratroopers they didn't have enough Medical Technicians to administer to all of the wounded. Kenneth was sent to Norville to help out. A steady stream of wounded soldiers came into the temporary Aid Station, Kenneth and the other medical personnel were working around the clock to administer to all the wounded. A heavy fog rolled into the area, this caused a pause in the fighting. A report was made that there was a wounded soldier who needed help on the outskirts of Norville. Kenneth was dispatched to look for him, Corporal Jennings went with him. Corporal Jennings was carrying a 30 caliber Browning Automatic Rifle (BAR). They were unable to find the wounded soldier in the fog. Suddenly the fog lifted, They looked up to see four German Soldiers standing in front of a hill looking back at them, the Germans were carrying M40 9 millimeter parabellium sub machine guns (burp guns). Ay first, the Germans just stared at the two Americans, then one fired his burp gun, Corporal

Jennings began firing his BAR at the Germans, sending blood and flesh flying against the hill, in seconds, the German Soldiers lay in a heap almost cut in half. Now that they could see, Kenneth and Corporal Jennings located the wounded soldier, who has a serious gash in his leg that was caused by a large piece of shrapnel. He had lost a lot of blood, Kenneth sprinkled powered sulfa on the wound, gave him a shot of morphine and applied a splint. They were able to get the soldier back to the Aid Station, there he was given blood plasma, but Kenneth knew that he needed more care than could be given at the Aid Station. Kenneth and other Medical Technicians loaded the most severely wounded men into an ambulance and Kenneth took them to a hospital in Bastogne; on the way the ambulance was hit with rifle and machine gun bullets but the ambulance was able to make it to Bastogne, some others were not so lucky, they were hit by artillery shells and the helpless patients were trapped in the burning vehicles. The red crosses on the ambulances made excellent targets.

Vince Speranza was a nineteen year old Paratrooper who was with the 501st Airborne, the 501st was dug in about four miles from Bastogne. Vince was ordered to go to Bastogne to get some batteries, he made it to Bastogne and procured some batteries. On his way back, he passed a Catholic Church that was being used as a hospital for the 501st Airborne. He went into the church and saw a patient that he knew and went over to talk to him, the wounded soldier asked him, "Can you get me something to drink"? Vince told him, "The city is surrounded and no supplies can get in, where am I going to get something for you to drink"? The soldier told him, "Go to a tavern". Vince told him, "Okay I will try", Vince found a tavern that had been hit by an artillery shell but he found some beer there, he filled his helmet with beer and took it back to the church. Vince became a folk hero for taking beer to the wounded soldiers, which he wasn't aware of until he went back sixty-five years later, and found the taverns serving beer in little helmets and "Airborne Beer" was being brewed in Belgium.

Men who were defending Bastogne at small towns were running out of supplies and ammunition and were being surrounded by the Germans, the only ones that survived were the ones that withdrew without being killed or captured. At Norville the shooting was picking up again, the town was being bombarded with tank and artillery shells and there was firefights all over the perimeter. The supporting artillery had fired all their ammunition, the heavy fog and stormy weather prevented them from getting supplies and ammunition with an air drop. Without artillery support, the 101st Airborne could not prevent the Germans from advancing into the city; the decision was made to withdraw to Foy, which was halfway to Bastogne, they left Norville before the Germans overran their position. They loaded the wounded soldiers onto any vehicle they could and left the village, which was a pile of rubble from all of the tank and artillery shells. When they reached Foy, The German soldiers were already there, they ambushed the America column; many of the Airborne Soldiers were either killed or captured, many of the vehicles in the convoy were destroyed, the lucky ones escaped the attack and moved on to Bastogne.

On December 26, 1944, elements of General George Patton's Third Army, spearheaded by Lt Colonel Creighton Abrams commanding the 4th Armored Regiment broke through the German lines, the first tank through was nicknamed "Cobra King". On December 27, 1944, General Taylor reached Bastogne with the 4th Armored Division and took command. The most famous quote of the battle came from 101st acting Commander, Brigadier General McAuliffe; when German General Luttwitz sent a request for the surrender of Bastogne, General McAuliffe sent a reply back, "Nuts". After The Americans penetrated the

German lines that had surrounded the city, the Germans were beat back and thanks to the brave men of the 28th Infantry Division, the 101st and 501st Airborne and the 969th Artillery Battalion, who fought to the last man, the Germans assault in the Ardennes was a failure and the last major German Offensive.

The 28th Infantry Division having suffered a devastating 15,000 casualties, withdrew to fortify. While they were leaving, Kenneth saw an emaciated Dachshund limping down the road looking for something to eat. He remembered hearing animals crying because they were trapped in burning buildings, He reflected, "It is a shame that animals as well as humans should have their world turned into an inferno because of a war started by the cupidity of men." By January 1945, the 28th Infantry Division had moved south, Kenneth was with the 109th Infantry Regiment, who had fought with the French 1st Army in the reduction of the "Colmar Pocket". This area was called the Colmar Pocket because this was the last area where a pocket of Germans were still occupying territory in France. The 109th Infantry Regiment was awarded the French Croix de Guerre for their actions in fighting the Germans, which led to the liberation of Colmar.

By February 1945, the 28th Infantry Division was in position along the Olef River. The Olef is a river of North-Westphlia, Germany that flows through the western part of the country. The unit that Kenneth was with moved on to the Rhine River, meeting resistance along the way. The Rhine River begins in the Swiss Canton of Graubunden and flows through Switzerland; Germany, Netherlands, France and Liechtenstein for 766.15 miles (1233 kilometers) and is part of the Seigfried Line. The Seigfried Line was a line of defensive forts and tank defenses, originally built by Germany in 1916-17 and stretches for 300 miles from Kleve, Germany to Wierlem Rhine near the border of Switzerland, it was rebuilt between 1938-40 and contained more than 18,000 pill boxes and tank traps. The soldiers of the 28th Infantry were not expecting much resistance once they reached the Rhine River, they were wrong! The Germans had regrouped and dug in. they ambushed the Americans and fierce fighting continued for five days. The Americans were greatly outnumbered and had no artillery support, when it became obvious that they were going to be overrun, they had orders to withdraw to the Olef River. The Germans were closing in and the American soldiers left in a hurry. Kenneth, who had been administering to wounded soldiers night and day was in a trench ditch and was too exhausted and weak to make it out of the trench. German soldiers moved into the area and some of them came to the top of the trench that Kenneth was in, one of them pointed his burp gun at Kenneth, who managed to roll over and see the Germans and thought, "I am going to die!" A German Medical Technician whose name was Wilhiem Krausse saw Kenneth's medical insignia and shouted, "Don't shoot him, he can help us!" Wilhiem was six feet tall, 180 pounds, with sandy hair and an aquiline nose. The Germans pulled Kenneth out of the trench and took him back to their camp.

It was two days before Kenneth could help Wilhiem, when he was able to, the two of them were kept busy the next four days patching up German soldiers. The Germans soon realized that Kenneth had skills far above the average Medical Technician and orders were given to protect him. On the seventh day that Kenneth was at the German's camp, Wilhiem called Kenneth aside and asked him, "Do you think that you can get us to the American lines?" Kenneth replied, "Yes I think that I can". Wilhiem was tired of the war and knew that the Germans were fighting for a pernicious and desperate cause. That night at 10;00 PM they left the German compound.

They were feeling their way along a path that Kenneth had walked on before on his way to the Rhine River; when they saw some flashlights ahead of them, they quickly hid in some bushes and remained very quiet while a German patrol passed by them. When the German patrol had passed, they continued on as quietly as they could. Dawn was breaking by the time they reached an area close to the Olef River. A German patrol saw them and started shooting. Kenneth and Wilhiem started running, but Kenneth was hit in the side by two 7.92x57 millimeter bullets from a Kar98K Mauser carbine. Besides bleeding from the wounds caused by the bullets, Kenneth had two broken ribs. With Wilhiem practically carrying Kenneth, they went as fast as they could to the American lines. The Germans knew that they were near the American lines and did not pursue them. When they arrived at the American lines, Kenneth shouted at some Military Police, (MPs) "Don't shoot I am an American!" When they reached the MPs, who saw the German Uniform, grabbed Wilhiem and whisked him away, Kenneth never saw him again. Kenneth was always sorry that he did not have a chance to thank Wilhiem for saving his life, but he was probably okay. A young German man whose name was Frederich Burke was a glider pilot for the Luftwaffe, when his glider crashed, he was captured and taken as a prisoner of war to the United States. After Frederich was released from prison, he became an American Citizen and joined the American Army. Frederich served with honor as a Huey Helicopter Pilot in Vietnam. Frederich was mentioned in Robert Mason's book "Chicken Hawk", which is about the war in Vietnam. The MPs took Kenneth to an Aid Station in the rear, where a pressure bandage was applied and he was given a morphine shot. Later, arrangements were made to evacuate Kenneth and two more wounded soldiers to the 279th Hospital in Wales, this was the second time that Kenneth had been there for treatment.

Once again he was treated with the strong tranquillizers nick named "Blue 88s". The soldier who was assigned to look after

Kenneth and help him with his daily activities was Edward N. Harvey, who was nick named "Tiny The Flash", stood about six feet tall and weighed 220 pounds and had a beautiful soprano voice and was the scintillating star of the "Govilon Gulch Flyers". Edward looked after Kenneth for two weeks.

As Kenneth ribs began to heal and he could do more things around the hospital, he began to help out with the other patients and eventually became a part of the hospital staff.

CHAPTER

Six

When Kenneth attended to each new wounded soldier, some with missing arms and legs, their minds shattered by their experiences along, with others that he saw, flashbacks of the horrors that he had experienced became more frequent and he became more depressed every day.

By June 3, 1945 the 279th Hospital and most of it's personnel, Kenneth among them, had moved to Berlin, Germany. The war in Germany was winding down but our armed forces were still very much into the war on the Pacific Front against the Japanese, there was talk that the 279th Hospital was going to move to the Asian front. That was too much for Kenneth, he already had enough of war. Kenneth had made friends with a patient whose name was Maurtz Milles who was from Sweden. Sweden is the third largest country in Europe, with 450,295 square kilometers, population 9.59 million and borders on Norway and Finland. Sweden bas a high standard of living and Stockholm is its capital.

Kenneth confided in Maurtz that he was going to leave, but he didn't know where he would go, Mauritz told him, "My parents would be more than happy for you to come to their house." Mauritz' parents lived in Sundsvall, located in Vasternorrland County, Sweden, Sundsvall covers 60 square miles (27.46 kilometers), population as of 2010 was 51,354.

Kenneth left the hospital and two days later and arrived at Mauritiz's parents house. Mauritz had notified his parents that Kenneth would be coming, when Kenneth arrived, he was greeted as if he was one of the family and they did everything that they could to make Kenneth feel at home. Mauritz's father was about five feet ten inches tall, with blue eyes and slightly thinning sandy hair, his mother was a handsome woman, with sparkling green eyes and blond curly hair, Kenneth wondered if the hair color came out of a bottle. They Invited him to eat with them, they had one egg and insisted that Kenneth eat it.

Kenneth stayed with the Milles for a week and then he began to fdeel as if he were a burden on them. He called the Commander of the 279th Hospital, the Commander who was well familiar with Kenneth's record told him, "I have placed you on administration leave, I expect you to be back here soon". Kenneth thanked the Commander and began his two day trip back to the 279th Hospital the next day.

Kenneth stayed with the 279th Hospital until he was discharged in Berlin. After he was discharged, he was hired by Civil Service to procure supplies for the 279th Hospital. He had a high rank and it was pretty pleasant work but, after four months he became tired of it and went back to Terre Haute, Indiana. He tried to have a relationship with his daughter, but her mother had poisoned her against Kenneth and she wouldn't have anything to do with him.

Kenneth divorced his wife and went to Atlanta, Georgia and enrolled in Emory University. Too much had happened to him since the last time that he was there, he couldn't concentrate on is studies, he tried hard but when he realized how poor his grades were going to be, he dropped out of college and went back to Terre Haute.

Kenneth opened a Photography Shop. Kenneth started participating in civic activities and became first aid chairman of the Terre Haute Chapter of the Emergency First Aid Detachment. Kenneth was a good photographer but, in his state of mind, he couldn't keep up with the business end of running the shop. He was losing money trying to keep the shop open and had to close the shop. He worked as a Private Detective for about six months, he was fairly successful but post traumatic syndrome was affecting him more and more. He realized that he needed someone to help him and went to live with his brother, Jack Anderson, in Corpus Christi, Texas.

Jack Anderson was an interesting person himself, he served twenty years in the United States Air Force and was in line for a top enlisted job in the Air Force but he couldn't take it. Muscular dystrophy was prevalent in his family and he became afflicted with it. His leg muscles were beginning to get weak and he was discharged with one hundred percent disability.

When he was discharged from the Air Force, he bought a house in Corpus Christi, Texas. He worked at Goad Cadillac for a few months until it became too difficult for him to walk and he had to quit, eventually he became bound to a wheel chair.

He lived in Corpus Christi for a few years and then decided to move to the Texas Hill Country, something that he had always wanted to do. He bought a piece of raw land in the Hill Country close to Kendalia, Texas; he had a beautiful log cabin house built on the land and turned the property into a beautiful place that rivals most parks. The Muscular Dystrophy Association did a documentary on Jack to show what someone can do, if the person has the desire and determination to do it, although the person may be handicapped with Muscular Dystrophy.

Jack couldn't walk, but he was tough, he had a three wheel recreation vehicle that he used to move around on his property, late one cold evening he was riding on a hill, when the recreation vehicle turned over, pitching him out on the ground. He couldn't walk, so all he could do was holler, but no one could hear him and he spent the night on the ground. One thing that helped him make it through the night was his herding dog "Lady", who lay by his side all night. The next morning, as people were going to work, Jack would holler and wave to them, some waved back and kept on going, finally a neighbor named Vogel saw him and came and got him up and helped him to get back into his house.. It became too difficult for him to get on his recreational vehicle so, he bought a golf cart, the golf cart had all hand controls, he used a sliding board that he placed from his wheel chair to the seat of his golf cart and then he would pull himself over. One evening he was driving his golf cart down by his pond, he drove under a cedar tree and a limb flipped him out into the pond, he couldn't get out of the pond, all he could do was yell and hope that someone would hear him, no one did and he spent the night in the water. The next morning a neighbor heard him yelling and came and got him out of the water.

Jack was the most incredibly generous person that I have ever known. One day I walked into his house and said, "Jack I need a thousand dollars", without saying a word, he pulled out his checkbook and wrote a check for a thousand dollars. I fell down thirty feet of concrete steps and busted my ankle pretty bad, which made it difficult for me to get around on my property, Jack knew that and gave me his golf cart. Jack helped many of his neighbors in any way that he could and kept on doing it until he passed away Christmas Eve 2011.

Kenneth lived with Jack for a few years before his health began to deteriorate. He went a to Veterans Administrations Hospital, where he was diagnosed with cancer, he was admitted to the hospital and stayed there for about a month. His brother came to check on how he was doing and discovered that nothing was being done for him, his brother immediately had him discharged from the hospital and took him to a doctor in Corpus Christi, Texas, who had him admitted in Spohn Hospital. Kenneth had a friend in Corpus Christi who came to visit him everyday, his friend worked at the Corpus Christi Army Depot; his friend would get on his motorcycle after work and ride to the hospital and shave Kenneth and do whatever else he could for him. When Kenneth was discharged from the hospital, his friend drove him back to his brother's house in the Hill Country.

Kenneth lived in the Hill Country with his brother until 1989 when his health got worse. Kenneth had two sisters, Mary and Elizabeth, who came and got him and took him back to Terre Haute, Indiana, where he passed away shortly after he arrived in Terre Haute, a true American Hero.

CREDITS

- The Longest Day by Cornelius Ryan
- World War II Day By Day by Donald Sommerville
- Alamo In The Ardennes by John C. McManus
- Beyond The Beachhead by Joseph Balkoski
- Russ Hauenstein

ABOUT THE AUTHOR

Jim Carter was born in Witchata Falls, Texas. He grew up in the Forth Worth, Texas area. He spent twenty years in the United States Navy. After he retired from the navy, he went to college and earned a Master's Degree in Psychological Counseling. He worked for fifteen years for Civil Service in three different Departments. He now lives in the Beautiful Texas Hill Country with his two dogs, a dachshund named Duke and a Terrier named Ashton. He is greeted every morning by deer, wild turkeys and many other species of birds. Besides novels, he writes short stories, essays and poetry.